How to Analyze People

Valuable Techniques on How to Interpret Body Language, Human Psychology, and Various Personality Types

Preface

This book: *"How to Analyze People: Valuable Techniques on How to Interpret Body Language, Human Psychology, and Various Personality Types Personality Types"* is intended for individuals who want to learn how to analyze people through their nonverbal and verbal cues.

If you want to learn the skill of human analysis, you can use the knowledge you would acquire from this book to improve and nurture your relationships, understand people's personality types, and acquire a positive frame of mind when dealing with people. This can lead to success and happiness in each of your endeavors.

To prevent ambiguity, the language used is simple and concise. Various examples and proven techniques are also given, so that you can practice the concepts properly and master the skill of analyzing people.

Continue reading this book and learn the skill of people analysis. Know how you can apply them properly, as well. Knowledge gained without application is not learning.

Thanks again for downloading this book. Have fun reading and learning!

The trademarks that are used are without any consent, and the publication of the trademark is without permission or backing by the trademark owner. All trademarks and brands within this book are for clarifying purposes only and are the owned by the owners themselves, not affiliated with this document.

Table of content

Contents

Chapter 1: Why You Need to Analyze People

Have you ever wondered what your purpose in life is? Surely, you had an inkling that you're here on earth not for yourself alone. Whether you like it or not, you live in a world where you cannot avoid being with people, because man, by nature, is a social being.

Since, this is an inescapable situation; you should make the best out of it. Hence, you need to learn how to be with people harmoniously and cultivate healthy relationships with others.

Why do you need to analyze people? This is a simple question that has a complex answer. You will find the answers in the pages of this book. However, let's establish the primary reasons why you have to embark on this quest.

A person who knows how to analyze people is more successful in their lives and relationships.

Reasons why you need to analyze people

1. **To understand people**

   You have to understand people so you can live with them harmoniously. If you don't have the skill to adapt to the society around you, your survival is in question. No man is an island. You would be living your life in loneliness and depression if you wouldn't want to associate with the people around you.

2. **To be able to understand people you must learn how to empathize with them**

   It would be difficult for you to understand people if you don't feel what they feel - if you don't empathize with them. Thus, you need to place your feet in their shoes.

3. To improve relationships

When you understand people, there will be less squabbles and enmity. Your relationships will improve and you will be happier and more fulfilled. Of what use is success at work when you're not happy? At the end of the day genuine success lies in your success with your relationships.

4. To succeed

If your relationships with other people are successful, you would be happier. The happier you are the more motivated and inspired you are to do all the things you want to do. With this positive frame of mind, you would certainly succeed in any undertaking you're bound to engage in.

5. To detect manipulation and lies

One advantage of being able to analyze people is to detect dishonesty. You don't expect people to lie to you all of the time, but it still wise to be cautious. If you learn to read people, you won't be subjected to lies and manipulations. You would be less susceptible to being conned. Wouldn't that be enough reason to motivate you?

6. To make friends

Even if you're an introvert, you would need friends every now and then. Knowing how to make loyal friends by learning how to analyze people is a wonderful skill you surely want to acquire.

7. To help people

You can help people, if you are able to analyze them. You can point them towards activities that would nurture their relationships; help them become successful in their careers; and turn them into better persons. You would come to know what help they need and how you can help them.

As you read the ensuing chapters, you would come to learn the noteworthy reasons why you need to learn how to analyze people.

Chapter 2: Understanding the Human Mind

The human mind (brain) is the most powerful organ in the human body. Only the human mind can rationalize, solve problems and perform cognitive functions that no other living being can do. This is the major reason why you differ from animals – you have a rational, thinking brain.

It's also the mind that allows you to perform all the cognitive, physical and emotional ideas that you have planned. Without the brain acknowledging your goal to analyze people, nothing would happen; your body won't act the way you want it to. This is because the brain is the center of the nervous system. Every act passes through the brain, and the brain has to trigger it to happen.

Formation of basic beliefs and thoughts

There are multiple factors that influence the way you think and the way your thoughts are generated. These factors start from the day you were conceived in the womb of your mother. Yes, that's right – as soon as the sperm cell penetrates the ovum, your "indoctrination" begins.

Various scientific studies established the connection between the mother's behavior and practices and the condition of the fetus. Undoubtedly, alcohol consumption, intake of prohibited drugs and smoking have detrimental effects on the fetus. These substances can damage the organs of the fetus - including the brain. The worst effect is for the baby to become a "blue baby" – dead at birth.

It was also observed that mothers who viewed their pregnancy negatively had a child who has "poorer emotional regulation and attention."

The role of heredity and environment in a person's mental abilities

When a person is born, there are two main factors that affect the growth and development of the baby. These are his genes and the environment in which he would thrive in.

You inherit your genes from both your father and mother, and these genes will leave a mark primarily on your physical, physiological attributes and mental abilities. You inherit your blood type, the color of your skin, eyes and hair. Your intellect is a combination of the IQ of your parents.

Thus, the mental capacity of a person comes also from his genes. The environment will then either hone or stymie the development of the person's intellectual abilities.

This is the reason why when judging a person; you have to consider his background and environment.

The environment as a crucial factor in the formation of a person's beliefs

The environment in which the individual has grown affects his way of thinking. If a person grew in a family where violence is a common occurrence, he will end up thinking violence is acceptable and is a common practice.

Another example is when a person is showered with love throughout his growing up years. He would naturally think that love is a given.

When he goes out into the world, he would later learn that there are people devoid of love, and that not every person would love him. This will also develop him into a good or bad person, depending on the support and advices that he would receive.

This is how your mind evolves and develops. Some people may be exposed to traumatic experiences, which would scar them for life and affect the way they think.

Most probably the person's beliefs would be something like, "People are unkind, so I have to protect myself at all times."

Power of the mind

However, as human beings, you have the power to create your own life. As the popular cliché goes, "Life is 10% of what happens to you and 90% of how you react to it." It's all about attitude. You must train yourself to stay firm and do something you plan to do, and not just flow with the water, wherever it may lead you.

Despite the role of heredity and environment, you still have the power to direct your life towards success and happiness.

How? By changing the way you think.

You want to analyze people? Then commit yourself towards this goal as if your life depended on it.

Believe that you can do it, and you can. You are what you think you are. Psyche yourself - every morning and evening - that you believe you would be able to accomplish the task. Look at yourself in the mirror and say, "I can read people's minds. I can read people's minds...I will succeed...."

Do this every day and soon your subconscious will catch on. When the subconscious becomes aware of your goal, together with your conscious mind, they will act together to help you succeed.

Of course, as you psyche yourself, you have to practice the skill. It's a skill so you can only acquire it, when you practice it.

It's like riding a bike. You can only learn how to ride a bike, if you actually ride one and practice.

In addition, you have to be aware that your mind is powerful and could affect your body's responses to certain events. Without your brain commanding your body, your body won't be able to move a muscle or lift a finger. That's how powerful your mind is.

Also, you have learned how the mind works and the reasons behind the thoughts and beliefs of people. Use this as a tool in reading and analyzing people.

Chapter 3: Analyzing Yourself to Analyze Others

What type of personality are you? Knowing who you are can be a crucial stepping stone to analyze people better. You cannot analyze people accurately, if you don't know yourself. This is because when analyzing people, you also bring yourself into the equation.

It's like when you see a glass which is half-full, your perception of the scene would be based on your personality. Are you an optimist or a pessimist? Do you see the glass as half-full or half-empty?

What are your core beliefs? Do you believe in God or a Supreme Being, or are you an atheist?

You have to get to know yourself first before you can analyze others. You can take the quiz to help you determine your personality type.

Quiz for personality analysis

Instructions:

Select the answer that best describes you. Don't leave any neutral and unanswered questions. You should answer all the questions based on your own perception and not on what you think other people would answer.

Select the choice that best describes the intensity of your action/reaction to the primary statement.

1. You tend to find opportunities in any given situation.
   a. Always
   b. Most of the time
   c. Sometimes
   d. Rarely

e. Never

2. You prefer to stay home and enjoy your time alone, rather than go to a party.
    a. Always
    b. Most of the time
    c. Sometimes
    d. Rarely
    e. Never

3. You solve problems following an established structure.
    a. Always
    b. Most of the time
    c. Sometimes
    d. Rarely
    e. Never

4. You prefer to learn from your own experiences than from books or notes.
    a. Always
    b. Most of the time
    c. Sometimes
    d. Rarely
    e. Never

5. You often feel lonely when you're in a crowd of people.
    a. Always
    b. Most of the time
    c. Sometimes
    d. Rarely
    e. Never

6. Your first impression of people is almost always correct.
    a. Always
    b. Most of the time
    c. Sometimes
    d. Rarely
    e. Never

7. You prefer to work alone in company assignments.
    a. Always
    b. Most of the time
    c. Sometimes
    d. Rarely
    e. Never

8. You decide based on what you feel, and not on what you think.
    a. Always
    b. Most of the time
    c. Sometime
    d. Rarely
    e. Never

9. It's best for you to work silently in the background than working in the limelight.
    a. Always
    b. Most of the time
    c. Sometime
    d. Rarely
    e. Never

10. You can predict future events, from out of the blue.
    a. Always
    b. Most of the time
    c. Sometimes
    d. Rarely
    e. Never

11. You can sense immediately whether a person is telling a lie or not.
    a. Always
    b. Most of the time
    c. Sometimes
    d. Rarely
    e. Never

12. Before you act, you take time to analyze the situation.
    a. Always
    b. Most of the time
    c. Sometimes
    d. Rarely
    e. Never

13. You want your activity to be organized and planned.
    a. Always
    b. Most of the time
    c. Sometimes
    d. Rarely
    e. Never

14. You find it exciting to embark on new endeavors.
    a. Always
    b. Most of the time
    c. Sometimes
    d. Rarely
    e. Never

15. When you witness an incident, you find yourself jumping to conclusions.
    a. Always
    b. Most of the time
    c. Sometimes
    d. Rarely
    e. Never

16. When watching someone recount his sad story, you find yourself crying.
    a. Always
    b. Most of the time
    c. Sometimes
    d. Rarely
    e. Never

17. You establish your goals first, before initiating an activity.
    a. Always
    b. Most of the time
    c. Sometimes
    d. Rarely
    e. Never

18. You follow standard procedures when working on a case.
    a. Always
    b. Most of the time
    c. Sometimes
    d. Rarely
    e. Never

19. During a conflict, you moderate the incident by the book.
    a. Always
    b. Most of the time
    c. Sometimes
    d. Rarely
    e. Never

20. You judge noisy people, instantly, as bad mannered.
    a. Always
    b. Most of the time
    c. Sometimes
    d. Rarely
    e. Never

21. In a new environment, you don't immediately adapt to the social circle.
    a. Always
    b. Most of the time
    c. Sometimes
    d. Rarely
    e. Never

22. You listen more than you speak.
    a. Always
    b. Most often
    c. Sometimes
    d. Rarely
    e. Never

23. You listen to what you heart tells you instead of your brain.
    a. Always
    b. Most often
    c. Sometimes
    d. Rarely
    e. Never

24. You would rather follow a trail when on a hike rather than explore.
    a. Always
    b. Most often
    c. Sometimes
    d. Rarely
    e. Never

25. You weigh the pros and cons of an issue before you decide.
    a. Always
    b. Most often
    c. Sometimes
    d. Rarely
    e. Never

26. You take things at face-value, life is short anyhow.
    a. Always
    b. Most often
    c. Sometimes
    d. Rarely
    e. Never

27. You don't want to dwell on a problem, you want to solve it immediately and move on.
    a. Always
    b. Most often
    c. Sometimes
    d. Rarely
    e. Never

28. You believe that every action has a corresponding reaction.
    a. Always
    b. Most often
    c. Sometimes
    d. Rarely
    e. Never

29. When a financial emergency occurs at home, you adjust to the situation promptly.
    a. Always
    b. Most often
    c. Sometimes
    d. Rarely
    e. Never

30. You don't easily panic. You remain calm amidst an emergency.
    a. Always
    b. Most often
    c. Sometimes
    d. Rarely
    e. Never

How to score your quiz

A = 5

B = 4

C = 3

D = 2

E = 1

Interpretation of Scores

These are the types of personalities focused on in each number. If you have scored highly in that particular number; then most likely, you're that type of person indicated in the number. Score yourself based on the traits.

Example: If you have scored 5 in all of the 'Sensing" statements; then consider it as one probable personality that you may have. The lower your score, the least likely you have that trait.

Add all your scores for each type:

1. Sensing - for question #1, it deals with the "Sensing" type, so, the person, who has a 'Sensing" type of personality would choose a = 5 points, or b = 4 points. The higher the score, the more likely the person is a "Sensing" personality. This goes true with the next questions.

2. Introversion

3. Judging

4. Intuition

5. Introversion

6. Intuition

7. Introversion

8. Feeling

9. Introversion

10. Intuition

11. Intuition

12. Perceiving

13. Judging

14. Feeling

15. Judging

16. Feeling

17. Thinking

18. Thinking

19. Thinking

20. Judging

21. Perceiving

22. Feeling/Perceiving

23. Thinking

24. Sensing

25. Perceiving

26. Perceiving

27. Feeling

28. Thinking

29. Sensing

30. Thinking/sensing

Example:

1. Sensing – you chose c, which is = 3
2. Introversion – you chose a = 5
3. Judging – you chose a = 5

You add up all your scores on "Sensing" (#1, #24, #29, #30), and that would be your total score. The personality type that will obtain the highest score would be your personality type.

Each personality type is assigned 4 questions. So, a perfect score would be 20 points for each of them.

Take note that there are no extroversion statements, because if the person is not an introvert, it's automatically concluded that he's an extrovert.

Now, that you have an idea of what type you are, you can incorporate this with the impression of other people about you, and with your own personal evaluation of yourself.

Identify your strength and weaknesses, and start from there. Boost your strengths and develop your weaknesses.

If you're ready, let's start the ball rolling on how to analyze people.

Chapter 4: Basics of Analyzing People

Now, let's go to the basics of analyzing people and how to figure the personality type of individuals you randomly meet.

<u>The basics of analyzing people are:</u>

1. **Physical make-up**

   The physical make-up of a person is one basic aspect that you should pay attention to. Simply observing the person can allow you to form a judgment of that person.

   This is called physiognomy, wherein the personality of a person is judged based on his external appearance or facial characteristics.

   - *Facial*

     Observing the facial bone's structure can help you analyze people. Reportedly, broad faces are considered manlier than narrower faces.

     It was observed that people with broader foreheads are more intelligent and resourceful.

     The shape of the face is also considered when analyzing people. A round face indicates generosity and kindness. A square face means that the person has splendid stamina and courage. An oval face means the person is amiable and tactful. A diamond face indicates that the person pay attention to details and is a perfectionist. A triangular face means that the person has the tendency to lead. A heart-shaped face indicates that the person is strong willed.

A high bridge nose exudes physical energy, while a flaring nose can mean the person is an irate. Typically, flat noses reflect poor energy but at the same time, harmony.

Look into the person's eyes and mouth corners and observe if there are any laugh lines. These are usually lines that indicate the person smiles often. The shape of his lips will also show this. If the corners of his lips are pointed downwards, the person has pouted most of the time, indicating that he is a grouchy and sad person. If the corners are going upwards, this means the person smiled often. Thus, he must be a jolly, happy, and cheerful person.

Observe the facial expression. You can find out instantly if the person is interested. If he smiles with his eyes, he is. If it's a false smile, his eyes won't light up. If he's pouting and angry, of course, he's not interested in you and what you're saying.

The crucial role of micro expressions

Beware of the micro expressions on a person's face. These are expressions that would suddenly flash on his face. If the person has superb control over his emotions, it would be difficult reading him, but you can, by keenly watching for his micro expressions. They can come out in a flash and be gone in seconds, so keep your eyes open. Examples of micro expressions are: a sudden quirk of the lips, a roll of the eyes, a pout, or a quick, angry stare. Focus on the eyes and the lips, where you can observe his micro expressions. These are the genuine expressions of his mood.

- *Body built*

Look at the person's body built. Does the person have atrophying or thin muscles? This indicates he doesn't exercise at all, and hence, he must be 'lazy' or uncaring about his health, or he's just too busy to exercise. You have to integrate your analysis with the other techniques of analyses to arrive at the correct one.

Is the person's body well-buffed and his muscles nicely-toned? If it is, then the person is a health enthusiast, who wants to stay healthy, fit and trim. So, you can conclude that the person is energetic and physically active.

- *Manner of walking*

Does the person walk with a swagger, walk confidently, walk dejectedly, or walk with indifference? You can notice if the person is confident when his shoulders are straight, his chest thrust forward and his steps certain.

He walks dejectedly when his shoulders are stooped, his steps faltering and slow. He walks with indifference when he walks by swinging his body and moves straight without bothering to see what, or who stands in his pathway.

These are all indications of the person's state of mind and personality. You certainly don't need to be a psychologist to read these physical actions.

- *Manner of sitting*

This is the same with the manner in which a person sits. Notice the position of his legs, his posture and the position of his body. If he sits on the edge of the chair, this means that he's nervous and anxious.

Likewise, when he fidgets in his chair and does leg jerks.

If he spreads his legs and sits straight and unmoving, he must be confident and unfazed - certain of himself and of his purpose.

Notice the gestures of his hand; is his finger busy toying with something? This can be his hair, the chair, or an item. This denotes that he is anxious.

Observe his torso. Where is it facing? Typically, the chest faces the direction of the person he is interested in. So, if the chest is towards you, it means he might be interested in you, or in what you're saying. If he twists his body away from you, it's a clear indication that he's not interested in you and what you're saying.

- *Posture*

A person's posture can speak volumes of the mood he is in, or even of his entire personality. A stooped figure can denote lack of self-confidence, and/or indifference.

The way he carries himself (poise) can also reflect his personality. You can observe people carrying themselves with elegance and you say, "Ah, that person is well-educated and is self-confident."

2. Personality types

For personality types you can simply classify people as introverts or extroverts; or according to their physical body types, or mental aptitudes (intelligent or dumb), or emotional state (indifferent or caring).

You can also refer to a more complex classification, the 16 personality types of Myers-Briggs as discussed in the next chapter (chapter 5).

3. Intuition

Intuition is one of the basic aspects of analyzing people because you can sense what you cannot actually see. You can train yourself to read people instinctively by practicing the skill every time you get the chance. Practice will help you acquire the skill eventually.

You can practice intuitive analysis on your family members and friends first, so you can check immediately if you were right with your intuition. Intuition plays a paramount role in analyzing people. Developing your intuition is discussed in chapter 12.

4. Verbal cues

Unless you know how to understand verbal cues correctly, you won't be able to read and analyze people. Verbal cues can be harder to read, because sometimes, people don't mean what they say. You will learn more about verbal cues in chapter 11.

5. Nonverbal cues

You can analyze a person through his nonverbal cues. The way he sits and stands, his facial expressions, the manner in which he behaves can tell you more than his verbal pronouncements. You will know more about nonverbal cues in the next chapters.

6. Nature of persons

You can view the nature of the person through his facial, verbal and nonverbal messages. Is the person naturally ill-tempered, or insouciant, or simply bad-mannered. The nature of the person can also depend on his growing up environment. It's not good to stereotype but you can, at least, have an idea of the person's nature through his background.

A person, who grew up in a convent must be naturally prayerful. A person who grew up amidst Mother Nature would most probably be a peace-loving person.

7. **Person's history**

This is one significant basic aspect of people analysis that you should know about. It can shed light into the person's behavior. Again, be careful in stereotyping; things may not be what they seem to be.

What type of family did the person come from? Where did he grow up? Where did he study? What were his influences during his growing up years? What's his guiding principle in life?

You can collate these data with the other information you have collected and use them all to come up with an accurate analysis of the person.

You can practice all of these basic aspects constantly, so that you can acquire the expertise in reading or analyzing people.

You can make predictions to practice the skill, and check afterwards if your predictions are correct. Try to predict patterns of individuals, or triggers that can cause a person to act the way he does.

It can be difficult at first, but as you get the hang of it, you would gradually become a master-reader of people.

Chapter 5: The Myers-Briggs Method of Determining Personality Types

Every individual possesses unique and different traits. His personality summarizes these characteristics and qualities, which give him a distinctive character that differs from others.

Carl Jung, who is a Swiss psychiatrist, introduced one of the earliest trait theories, which characterizes the way how every individual perceives, believes, feels or acts.

His Theory of Psychological Types demonstrated how consistency and uniformity exists even if there is variation and difference in a person's behavior.

To comprehend this theory, Katharine Cook Briggs and her daughter Isabel Briggs Myers developed the Myers-Briggs Type Indicator (MBTI) instrument.

Myers and Briggs concentrated on two (2) objectives in developing and applying the MBTI instrument:

1. To identify the basic preferences of each of the four (4) dichotomies mentioned in the theory of Carl Jung; and
2. To identify and describe the sixteen (16) distinctive personality types resulting from the interactions among the preferences.

Dichotomy is the difference or variation between two (2) things that are presented as being opposite or entirely dissimilar.

The basic preferences in each of the four (4) dichotomies are presented as follows:

1. **Extraversion versus Introversion**

Extraversion is when a person prefers to act and function in the external and outer world. Extravert people are more oriented to action.

While in *Introversion*, the person tends to focus in his own inner world. Introverts are thought-oriented.

2. Sensing versus Intuition

Sensing people identify information from senses. They see everything as simple and concrete.

Meanwhile, people who depend on intuition, also called *Intuiting* people, work out and understand by instinct. They tend to interpret and add meaning to the information they take in. Intuiting people are often artistic.

3. Thinking versus Feeling

A *Thinking* person establishes decisions on the basis of thinking. They focus on reasoning, logic, consistency and step-by-step problem solving.

Feeling people base their decisions on their feelings. They first look at the needs of the people and the circumstances, and then they tend to associate and empathize with the situation.

4. Judgment versus Perception

Those who are neat, orderly, and hard-working, always on time and schedules things carefully are people who base their decision on *Judgment*. They always prefer to decide on things.

Perceiving people or those who decide based on *Perception* are more spontaneous. They do things as the spirit moves them but they tend not to get things done. They are open to new information and options.

Myers- Briggs Type Indicator (MBTI) instrument

The Myers-Briggs Type Indicator (MBTI) instrument has been created to make individuals understand Carl Jung's psychological types theory and to help them understand their own behavior as well as others.

The MBTI is a psychometric personality test designed to measure an individual's psychological preferences on how he generates decisions and discern his surroundings. It is a test that is very popular and it is the most widely used personality assessment in the world.

This instrument is widely and popularly used in methods of teaching and academic subjects (pedagogy), career and marriage counseling, team building and group dynamics, professional and personal development, and others.

From the individual's preference in each category of the four (4) dichotomies, he may now have his own personality type which is assigned and expressed in a four-letter abbreviation. Below each MBTI type are the enumerated descriptions of the individual's personality:

Introversion (I) - Extraversion (E)
Sensing (S) – Intuition (N)
Feeling (F) - Thinking (T) –
Judgment (J) – Perception (P)

1. **Introversion (I), intuition (N), feeling (F), perception (P) - INFP**

    This type enjoys writing, creativity and language, ideas; is compassionate and caring; idealistic and pursues harmony at all cost; independent but is empathic and intuitive. Also, he relishes independence and is adaptable to any given situation.

2. **Introversion (I), sensing (S), feeling (F), judging (J) - ISFJ**

This person is considered as a stable, practical and sympathetic person. He can be quietly warm, caring, helpful and dependable. He is conservative, but you would be surprised at how detailed, systematic, organized and realistic he is. He wants to deal only with facts in a thorough manner.

3. **Introversion (I), sensing (S), thinking (T), perception (P) - ISTP**

This person is adventurous and is curious about a variety of activities. He adapts readily to situations because he's realistic, practical and a problem-solver. This is because of his analytical and exact mind. He's logical, independent and wants to participate in activities, hands-on.

4. **Extraversion (E), intuition (N), thinking (T), judging (J) - ENTJ**

This type of personality wants to plan and organize first before commencing the activity. But once he does, he's decisive, assertive, focused and would logically seek achievement and improvement. He may be critical at times but his systematic approach to activities usually makes him succeed.

5. **Extraversion (E), intuition (N), feeling (F), perception (P) - ENFP**

This type is playful and child-like. He is enthusiastic and imaginative about everything. He's often open, spontaneous, warm and insightful. Although he's individualistic, he's caring and is optimistic about life. He welcomes change and novelty.

6. Introversion (I), sensing (S), feeling (F), perception (P) - ISFP

This person has most of the traits that people would desire in a partner. He's caring, gentle, loyal, patient, adaptable, and helpful. He's also compassionate, observant, and idealistic.

7. Extraversion (E), sensing (S), thinking (T), perception (P) - ESTP

If you're the adventurous type, you would love spending time with this type of person because he's adventurous, active, easy going and loves seeking excitement. He's observant, analytical, but realistic too. He easily adapts, and would act as a peace-maker during trouble. He works efficiently, as well.

8. Extraversion (E), sensing (S), feeling (F), judging (J) - ESFJ

He's empathic; hence, is warm, sociable, caring, appreciative and loyal. He loves being around people and find ways to harmonize relationships and empathize with them. He's conscientious, responsible and practical.

9. Introversion (I), sensing (S), thinking (T), judging (J) - ISTJ

This type of person works efficiently and in an organized and systematic manner. He's the practical type who logically analyzes and solves problems in detail. He doesn't accept things as is but goes into the details and views the facts. But once he makes decisions, they are decisive. He's a stable and a responsible person you can rely on.

10. **Extraversion (E), sensing (S), thinking (T), judging (J) - ESTJ**

He acts as the leader, who organizes systematically, and asserts his role. He's logical, practical, critical, and uses a lot of common sense in obtaining the results he wants.

11. **Extraversion (E), intuition (N), feeling (F), judging (J) - ENFJ**

He's warm, tactful and a harmonizer because he loves being in the social circles. He's empathic, conscientious and idealistic. He knows how to express himself well, and has great imagination. He's also appreciative of other people's concern and help.

12. **Extraversion (E), intuition (N), thinking (T), perception (P) - ENTP**

This person loves independence, theoretical, abstract, analytical and complex cases. He's creative too and adaptable. He welcomes novelty and is energetic and enthusiastic about life. He expresses himself well in any given situation.

13. **Introversion (I), intuition (N), thinking (T), judging (J) - INTJ**

This type of person relishes staying in one corner to conceptualize his ideas. He's independent and insightful and is critical and logical. He wants to understand as well as to be understood. He decides decisively without hesitation.

14. **Introversion (I), intuition (N), feeling (F), judging (J) - INFJ**

This type of personality is quiet but sensitive and inspiring. He's also inclined to be creative, insightful, and serious. He wants to be in harmony with other people and is persevering in pursuing his goals.

15. **Introversion (I), intuition (N), thinking (T), perception (P) - INTP**

He's independent and adaptable, just like most introverted persons. He wants creating things and is detached and complex at times. He desires pursuit of knowledge and is curious, logical, analytical, and critical in acquiring information.

16. **Extraversion (E), sensing (S), feeling (F), perception (P) - ESFP**

He's energetic, wants excitement, fun and spontaneity in his life. He adapts easily to the environment and to people because he's sociable, friendly, generous, and caring. You can rely on him because he's resourceful, observant, practical and adaptable. When he participates in activities, he wants a hands-on participation.

In using this instrument, there is no best type. All of the types are equal. The objective in knowing an individual's personality type is to understand and appreciate their differences.

MBTI does not measure an individual's character, ability or trait. It is different from other psychological and personality tests.

For the past forty (40) years, MBTI has been proven to be a valid and reliable instrument.

Chapter 6: Figuring the Personality Type of People

How can you figure the personality type of people? As previously explained, you can do this by applying the basic aspects of analyzing people discussed in chapter 4. You have to gather all the information derived from the basics and come up with a conclusion. But how can you actually do it?

<u>Here are steps on how to do it</u>

Step #1 – Create your first impression

This is the impression that you obtain just by looking at the person and analyzing him based on his facial expressions, verbal and nonverbal cues, body language and your intuition. Notice the way he dressed, his shoes, his style of hair, his perfume, and all the seemingly trivial things that you can observe. All these can tell you about the person.

An example is when he has dressed sloppily; this is an indication that he's careless and not properly prepared for the event. He may consider the event insignificant.

You can sum up all your observations and come up with the person's analysis. The role of first impressions is discussed in the next chapter (chapter 6).

Step #2 – Interact with the person

Try to interact with the person to find out how he behaves with other people. If you cannot, you can observe how he interacts with the people within his vicinity. Notice his verbal and nonverbal language. Does he act according to the first impression that you had of him? Were you correct in your first analysis? Adjust your conclusions, or confirm your conclusions accordingly.

Step #3 – Learn about his background

You can drop a question here and there, unobtrusively, and in a tactful manner. You're not an FBI agent spying around other people. An example is this: "Oh, I guess you went to the same school as Mr. _____. You're attending the same event." The answer of the person can provide you a 'snippet' of information. A harmless question here and there will provide you some of the data you need to help you analyze the person.

Step #3 – Form your final analysis

After gathering all the information you can get your hands on, you can now form your final analysis of the person's personality. Use all the methods mentioned in the previous chapters (example - Myers-Briggs). Naturally, you may not be able to be spot on in your analysis of some individuals, but as you practice your skills, you would progressively master it.

Step #4 – Determine if you have successfully analyzed the person

This can happen over a period of time as you come to know the person more. But if you were not given the chance to prove your analysis, then that's fine. It's not the end of the world. You can always meet someone whom you can apply all of the steps mentioned here.

These are the steps that you can follow when you want to figure out the personality type of the person.

Chapter 7: The Role of First Impressions

You usually form your first impressions based on your five senses: what you see, hear, taste, feel, and smell. Observing the person through these senses and the help of intuition, you can successfully create first impressions accurately.

To some people, first impressions are vital because of the following reasons:

- **They are lasting**

   You're familiar with the concept that 'first impressions last'. This can be true in some instances, but not altogether applicable in situations where you can be with the person for a longer period of time. Over the course of getting to know the person, your first impression may totally change.

- **They are usually correct**

   Some experts stated that first impressions tend to be highly accurate, especially if the analyzer had some background in reading persons. Nevertheless, you cannot categorically conclude that this happens all of the time.

- **They are the bases of future predictions**

   You can store in your memory your first impression of a person and observe his future behavior if this coincides with your first impression.

Whatever reasons people have, first impressions are considered essential during job interviews where you have to put your best foot forward. Certainly, you have to do this if you want to land the job. Dress right, speak confidently (even if your knees are trembling), look at your interviewer eye to eye, and sit up straight - but at the same time - stay relaxed in your chair.

If you're in the shoes of the job interviewer, take note of micro expressions, and nonverbal or body language. Use your intuition. Job applicants will always try to impress you. Hence, be smart to differentiate, which actions are genuine, and which ones are not.

You can acquire the skill of reading people on first sight by being observant. Practicing the skill every day will help you hone it.

Chapter 8:   Reading or Analyzing Body Language

Body language or nonverbal language speaks more of the person's true feelings and thoughts than verbal language. A person can lie verbally, but he cannot truly hide his body language.

Also, you must bear in mind that to every rule there will always be an exception. Thus, you have to know the background, culture, personality of the person you're talking to, and the instances in which the act was performed before you should judge his body language.

An example is: when a person is shivering because of cold weather and not because he's nervous.

<u>Here are some body languages and what they mean:</u>

Eye contact

The eyes are thought to be the windows of your soul. Your eyes can speak volumes of what you feel. You can look into a person's eyes and tell instantly what he feels.

> ➢ *Good strong eye contact* – When a person meets your eye, it shows that she has self-confidence, and is telling the truth. Obviously, there are exceptions to the rule, such as in cases of pathologic liars, who can lie straight to your face - without batting an eyelash.
>
> There are also some instances in different cultures, when staring is considered bad manners (Western culture), while in the East, staring naturally occurs without any offense intended. Hence, the person may avoid your gaze.

So, you have also to consider the background of the person you're talking to. His background has molded his behavior and body language.

You will know when the person you're talking to isn't interested in what you're saying if he doesn't look at you and his body is veered away from you.

It's a sign of interest when you look at the person when he talks, as well, but don't overdo it. Staring at him after the conversation when he's busy with other activities is considered rude.

Legs

> A man who spreads his legs wants to establish his dominance.

> Locked ankles in males and females denote nervousness, apprehension, anxiety and a way of protecting themselves from external dangers.

> A female who crosses her legs and wraps her feet around her ankles signifies nervousness and anxiety.

> A female who crosses her leg and allows them to be parallel to each other can mean she's relaxed or confident.

> A female who holds her hair in one hand and curls her hair with another hand may indicate nervousness more than flirtation. Sometimes, it can be mistaken as being flirtatious.

> A female playing with her hair, spreading it away from her face indicates she's flirting and is open for relationships.

- ➢ A female who tosses her head and shakes her hair is also considered flirtatious. Curling her hair around her fingers is also a sign of flirtation. The flirting person mimics the other person's posture.

Nails

- ➢ Nail biting usually indicates nervousness, stress and anxiety.

Arms

- ➢ Crossed arms can indicate various things. It can mean that you're not welcome to his territory, or that he's not interested in you, or that he's being defensive.

- ➢ When the arms are crossed behind his back, this action can indicate hesitation or shyness.

- ➢ Arms akimbo denotes that the person wants to establish his dominance and authority.

- ➢ Arms at the back of the head, with the hands interlocked and supporting the head, indicate the same meaning as arms akimbo.

Palms

- ➢ Rubbing the palms together means that the person is expecting something good. He's being hopeful and optimistic.

Chest

- ➢ The direction in which the chest is pointing will denote where the person's interest lies.

Hand shake

- ➢ The meaning of a handshake will depend on the strength and warmth of the grip. The stronger and warmer the grip is, the more interested the person is in you.

- ➢ Handshakes, where both hands are used, can denote commitment and desire for closeness, or dominance.

- ➢ Hands on cheek – the person is thinking, reminiscing

Standing

- ➢ Standing away from the person – when the person stands away from you, it means he's not interested in you as a person, and in what you're saying.

- ➢ Standing close to you – when the person does this, he's interested in you and he wants to hear what you have to say.

Sitting down

- ➢ This is true also when sitting down. A disinterested person will stay away from you, as far as possible. Placing a distance between you and him; ensures the person that he can pretend not to notice you.

Take stock of the situation, and evaluate before you judge. Perhaps, he's interested in you but you don't smell good? That's something to think about. Or you have forgotten to change your clothes. Explore other reasons first before arriving at any conclusion.

Fingers

- ➢ Finger tapping – nervousness and impatience

- ➤ Finger 'steepling' – fingertips are placed together to show that the person is in control, and wants to assert his authority.
- ➤ Finger drumming – anxiety, impatience, nervousness

Head

- ➤ Nodding the head means the person is agreeing with what's being said.

- ➤ Shaking – means the opposite; it can also indicate disbelief or non-acceptance.

- ➤ Bowed head – the person may be ashamed, shy, or wants to show that he recognizes your authority. He may also want to show obedience.

- ➤ Upward tilted head – if it's for a short time, it indicates that the person may be interested in what he just heard. So, he's trying to listen more attentively.

- ➤ Upward tilted head – for a longer period of time, denotes the opposite. The person finds the activity boring, or that he has lost interest in it.

Way of dressing

Here are some clothe styles and their possible meaning:

- ➤ Baggy clothes – depressed, not happy about his/her figure

- ➢ Sexy clothes – wants affirmation of her/his physical traits, wants to find partners, feels good about him/herself, wants approval
- ➢ Formal clothes – wants business relationships, wants everything to be organized and spot on.
- ➢ Bright-colored outfits – love for independence, carefree, happy, loves attention
- ➢ Dull-colored outfits – depressed, miserable, wants to lie low, uncomfortable in the lime light
- ➢ Flashy outfit – wants to be noticed and acknowledged, wants to be different, wants to establish his/her own identity.

If the person doesn't dress according to his/her age, it denotes that he/she wants to reminisce that phase of his/her life.

An example is an old woman dressing as a teenager. This can mean that she misses her teenage life and wants to remember it.

These are only some of the body languages that you can use to analyze a person's personality. There are thousands of body languages that you may want to study. You could also write down your own observations and create a logbook of these body languages for your future use.

Chapter 9: How to Detect If a Person is lying

To be able to read people correctly and analyze them properly, you have to learn how to reconcile their words with their actions. By doing this, you can also detect whether a person is lying or not. You can follow these steps to find out.

Step #1 – Listen to his words

Try to understand what the person is saying. You may want to take note mentally of his salient points. In addition, you can ask follow-up questions to clarify ambiguities.

Step #2 – Observe his nonverbal cues

Normally, a person who is honest can look at you straight in the eye, while he speaks. On the other hand, a person who is lying cannot meet your gaze. His eyes are unsteady and would look at something else when you try to connect with your eyes. Of course, the pathologic liar is an exception; he can look at you in the eye and still be able to spout his lies.

Look for those micro expressions that are almost imperceptible. A flash of scorn in his eyes can tell you that he may be fabricating falsehood out of his scorn for you.

Possible signs that a person is lying

- Lack of eye contact
- Dry mouth observed by his tongue licking his lips
- Fidgeting
- Eyes are everywhere
- Voice is low
- Voice quivers
- Uses words, such as "I don't know", "I'm not sure", "Perhaps", or "Most likely"

Step #3 – Do a simple test

Ask various questions and notice how he reacts to the facts and to the lies. Make this as a gauge to find out, which among his statements are true or not.

Examples:

Ask questions you know the correct answer to:

"So, are you living in the suburbs?"

You know he does, but you're asking anyhow. Observe his eye and mouth movement and his body language.

"Are you still attending your yoga classes?"

Again, observe his facial and body language

Next, ask questions that are lies and observe his facial and body language.

Examples:

"Some people saw you at the beach yesterday, is that true?"

"Are you an atheist?"

Observe how his facial expressions change, and how his body reacts to the statements. Obviously, the next statements should be prevarications, so you can observe how his face and body reacts to falsehood (lies).

Use his nonverbal reactions - that you have observed - to your true and false statements to gauge the veracity of his previous or ensuing declarations.

Step #4 – Collate your observations

You can now collate your observations mentally (if you don't have a chance to do it in writing). Focus more on the nonverbal language because these actions can rarely be falsified. They should be of paramount importance in your decision, whether the person is lying or not.

As you learn how to use this technique, you will become quicker in rendering your judgment. You can tell immediately whether the person is honest or not. It's a skill that's worth acquiring because you can use this skill at home, at work, and in business. You could also use this skill in analyzing people.

Chapter 10: Understanding Verbal Communication

Verbal communication is essential to relay a message to your audience. If you are working in a company, you need to use words with pitch and tone that is suited to what you want to express. The tone of your voice can trigger hurt or start an argument.

On the other hand, it can prompt the feeling of joy and acceptance. If you're in business, the tone of your voice used in dealing with your clients can either make or break you.

In communication, there are essential things that you need to know, if you are to improve your verbal communication skills as a person, or a company. If you are into business: the tone of your voice, your body language, voice pitch, speech pattern and the words you used must be appropriate.

#1- Tone of voice

The tone of voice is important in verbal communication. Here are the why tone is important:

Defines you as a person

The tone of your voice says a lot about your feelings and current state of emotions and about your personality. If you are dealing with the elderly, your tone can be warm and friendly. If it is the professionals you are faced with, you may need to be authoritative and confident. If you're in conversation with kids then it could be something light and simple.

The tone of your voice affects your customers or the people you get in touch with. They conjure up an image to attach to the voice. Your tone defines who you are to the people around you. The type of tone you use determines the image that people make of you.

Fosters trust

An appropriate tone of voice builds trust and confidence. When your voice exudes warmth, people tend to be drawn to you, and with time, comes trust.

Identifies you as a person

Although the tone of your voice is influenced by your feelings and emotions at any given time, it is how you deal with that emotion that counts. When you are frustrated, the tone of your voice in a conversation will tend to be argumentative, and the person you're talking to would feel it. Once you unleash those emotions, they would manifest in your tone of voice and people would notice it. People form their impressions on what they hear or see. They may brand you as a freak, or a weirdo.

On one hand, if you communicate with humor, warmth and light-heartedness, you draw people to you. They will look at you as someone easy to be with. This tone of voice sets you apart from the crowd. If you're a businessman, then you would keep your customers with you. With the appropriate tone of voice, you will stand-out from your competitors.

Critical ingredient of persuasion

When trust is established between you and the people around you this can be a powerful vehicle for understanding.

#2 - Words used to communicate

When you communicate, you want the person to understand the message you are relaying. You can only do that when you use words that are clearly understood by the receiver of the message. The words you use in communicating must mean the same with that of the recipient of the message.

#3 - Body language

Body language is a non-verbal communication channel but is essential to the verbal communication. It could happen that you're saying yes but your body language says no. Be careful with your body language. Some people could sense if something is amiss through the signals that your body exudes during a conversation. You may not realize it, but it does.

#4 – Voice pitch

The inflection of your pitch during verbal communications may affect the mood of the people involved in the conversation. Pitch is affected by your emotions. When you are excited, the pitch goes higher. When you're relaxed you're pitch would go lower.

It's important to manage your emotions to avoid inflections that may be misconstrued. You have to modulate your voice for effective communication.

Here's how to manage your pitch:

> **Manage your emotions well**

When you're angry, your pitch rises, and when it is high, it may be construed as annoyance with your audience. Try to calm down and relax, so that your larynx is not taxed.

> **Talk slowly**

To avoid nervousness when talking with a crowd, you should speak slowly, so that you can get your message across your audience successfully. When you're nervous, the tendency is for your pitch to rise a notch higher.

You're not prohibited from stressing a point. When you emphasize something in your speech, your pitch rises and other people might interpret it as anger.

#5 – Speech pattern

Accent is also essential in communication. Pronunciations are significant components of verbal communication. There are varied speech patterns that can ruin a conversation, such as:

Creaky voice

Most people are annoyed hearing a creaky voice. In business, it can ruin your opportunity to do business with your prospective clients. It may elicit a negative image for your company.

Inaccurate pronunciation

Correct pronunciation is critical in verbal communication. It creates a good impression of yourself with people in the conversation. It fosters a bond between you and the other person.

Inaccurate pronunciation results to people losing interest in your topic, forming a negative impression about you as a speaker, and they would tend to misunderstand your message.

You can call a verbal communication a success when the sender (coder) uses a language that's understood by the receiver (encoder). Thus, success would be accomplished when the message from the sender is understood clearly by the receiver.

Chapter 11: How to Do Cold Reading

Cold reading is typically performed by self-proclaimed psychics. Nonetheless, science has proven that there are still no proven psychics based on scientific experiments under controlled conditions.

Anyhow, cold reading would help practice your skill in analyzing people, thus you can perform this activity in your own home. You can do cold reading sans the fanfare and tarot cards, just to set the mood. You can pretend to be a psychic, for the moment. You can continually develop your so-called psychic skills and be tagged a psychic, if you wish.

The 'psychic' derives his fortune-telling or future predictions from a keen observation of the person's entire personality and information from the person himself to come up with his predictions.

You can practice cold reading with your family and friends to hone your ability in analyzing people. It's the same with practicing how to read and analyze people, only, you will be setting the appropriate atmosphere. Before you do it, you must have a positive frame of mind and the proper amount of self-confidence.

<u>Here's how you can do it.</u>

Step #1 – Set up a comfortable area in your house

You may want to use a cozy room or area in your house, where you can remain undisturbed. You may use dim light to make the atmosphere 'mysterious" to set the mood. Ascertain that the room temperature is not so cold or too hot.

Step #2 – Make use of tarot cards or similar materials

This will lend an atmosphere of mystery and supernatural to the room. The tarot cards can give you time to organize your thoughts, while you're deciding what to say.

Step #3 – Observe the person's physical appearance

As soon as the person enters, observe how he is dressed; is he dressed meticulously or not? Are there missing buttons? Or is his shirt not ironed? Does he smell good, or does he smell sweaty? Are his shoulders slumped? Does his body look fatigued? Did he walk in confidently, or were his steps wavering? How is he seated, is he fidgeting in his chair, or is he seated calmly?

From these observations, draw a swift, temporary conclusion.

Example:

If he's dressed sloppily, and came in with his shoulders sagging, you can conclude that he must have a problem at home. No one has attended to his clothing, and he appeared depressed. If it was a problem at work, he would be properly dressed but depressed (sagging shoulders).

Step #3 – Observe his facial expressions

You can look at his face, while stating your initial observation: *"There seems to be a problem at home…,"*

Apparently, the person would be surprised that you know what his problem is before he could even open his mouth.

Then, you can ask him to tell you what his concern at home is all about. Take note of the key points that you should remember.

He tells you about his concerns, and asks you what can happen in the future.

According to some scientist, psychics cannot truly see the future. Their predictions are based on educated guesses. So, that's what you will do yourself. Predict the future making use of what you have observed so far from the person himself.

Let's say, the person revealed that he had a big fight with his wife because he insisted that she should resign from her job.

As he's talking, observe his physiognomy; the shape of his face, his chin, his nose, his jaw, his lips, and the lines on his face. What do they tell about him? What is his type of personality? Refer to the previous chapters for this information.

Step #4 – Predict the person's future

After his revelation, you can start riffling the tarot cards as you organize your thoughts. You may want to ask him to draw a card, or two cards, while you're thinking. You have to learn a little bit about the meanings of the tarot cards, so you can associate them with your prediction.

Based on the techniques presented in this book, about the meaning of the shape of his face, his jaw, his lips, determine his personality. Is he a determined person, who can pursue his goals relentlessly? If he is, then most probably, they would get back together and stay together. Thus, you can predict his future along these lines.

Or, does he have a personality that is not adaptable? If this is the case, you could predict that, chances are, they would eventually go their separate ways.

It's not rocket science to read and analyze people, and in some way or another predict what could happen to them in the future.

However, you must inform the person that his future can change depending on what he does in the following days to come. Inform him that he has the free will to choose, and that he should control events he can (his relationship with his wife), but must not worry about events he can't control (weather, traffic, thoughts of other people).

That's the power of the human mind! The mind can 'command' the body.

If you were cold reading a family member or a friend, try not to use your previous impressions of him; instead use only the impressions you get from the activity itself. It would be difficult, but take note that you're only practicing your skill in analyzing people on the first meeting.

By reading and interpreting every aspect of the person's physical appearance, statements and body language, you can correctly analyze the personality of the person.

You have been provided a number of ways on how to analyze people. Now, all you have to do is put these methods into practice.

Chapter 12: Proven Techniques: Developing Your Third Eye or Intuition

All individuals have third eyes; only, the levels of their intuitions vary. Some may have fully developed theirs, while others ignored their intuitions altogether. This intuitive ability is also a skill that can be developed and acquired. This is one power that comes from your brain (mind). Without your human mind's commitment, you won't be able to do the following techniques.

You can cultivate your third eye too through constant practice. First, you can practice on inanimate things, such as cards, or images.

Materials

> Deck of cards
> Images or pictures

Step #1 – Spread the cards on the table and touch each one of them lingeringly.

Step #2 – Feel in your hands the sensations you get when touching the red cards. Remember these feelings.

Step #3 – Do the same with the black cards. Pass your fingers through the card and remember the sensation. At first, you won't be feeling anything, but with practice, you would learn to 'sense' the difference.

Step #4 – Separate the cards according to their suits. Separate the spades, clubs, hearts and diamonds and feel each of them in your hands. Close your eyes and touch each card with your fingers. Run your fingertips across the face of the card and try to feel the sensations.

Take note if there are differences with what you feel when you're touching the different card suits. You can do this until you have acquired certain sensations related to the cards.

Step #5 – Now, mix the cards and spread them on a clean table - face down. Try guessing the card based on how they feel in your hands, or on the sensations you experience as you touch them.

First, guess whether the card is black or red. You would be lucky if you can guess at least 3 to 5 cards correctly.

You're on the roll as a potential 'reader', if you can guess correctly 10 or more cards.

Keep doing this to practice your prediction and 'reader' skills.

Step #6 – Guess the specific cards. This is a Herculean task that may take a lifetime to acquire. But when there's a will, there's a way. You can do it. Remember, the power of the mind? The power of your mind combined with your developing skills can do wonders. Never give up until you have succeeded.

Just like the other skills, it takes practice to master the skill. Practice constantly.

Step #6 - Let a friend or family member choose 10 random images. Instruct him not to show the images to you. Instead, he holds the back of the image towards you, one by one.

Step #7 – Guess what the image is just by looking at the person's face and the back of the image. If you can guess even one of these images, you're awesome! You have a good future in analyzing people.

Do these several times until you can guess at least 30 cards, and 8 out of 10 pictures.

Take note that you can practice your skill even while at work, or while doing your chores. Observe people and then predict their next moves. Use all the skills you have learned from this book, and you will surely succeed in reading and analyzing people.

Chapter 13: Role of Transactional Analysis

Transactional analysis can be utilized, as well, when analyzing people. This stems from the fact that transactional analysis is related to how people behave. Sigmund Freud had categorized an individual's personality into three aspects: the Id, the Ego and the Superego.

According to Freud, the Id pertains to the emotional or irrational aspect of the mind, while the Ego is the rational or thinking aspect, and the Superego is the moral or spiritual aspect.

The concept was developed by psychotherapists and experts and is now considered as an essential part of psychology and human interaction.

The concept now has identified the three aspects of an individual's personality into the following:

> **Id** – child
>
> **Ego** – Adult
>
> **Superego** – Parent

Most conversations done are between two adults, and some are parent-child, and adult-child.

What is Transactional Analysis (TA)?

It is the study of human interaction; how each individual behaves with other individuals. Each communication between persons is considered a 'transaction'. When one person recognizes the other person, it's called a 'stroke'.

What are the roles of TA in analyzing people?

- When you're analyzing people's personalities, it helps identify the parent, adult or child in the person. This will help in his analysis.

- During conversations, you would know, which aspect of his personality has taken over, and this would point to the appropriate direction that you could initiate.

  An example is when the person is behaving as a child; you can then behave as the parent.

  Through his child-like behavior you can learn about his fears and secret aspirations and other aspects of his personality that are not visible in his adult self.

- It helps identify the facial expressions by considering these as more significant than verbal communication.

In Transactional Analysis, the verbal pronouncements are the least significant in interpreting statements during a conversation. What counts the most are the way the words were said, and the facial expression in which they were said.

Chapter 14: Cultivating Empathy to Understand People

People have an inherent trait of being empathic; nonetheless, many people don't use it frequently, so they forget how it feels to empathize. Empathy is one trait you have to cultivate to help you understand people more. This characteristic will play a crucial role in your quest of analyzing people.

What is empathy?

Empathy is the ability to truly feel what another person is feeling. It's the skill to put yourself in the other person's shoes. In other words, you're able to wear his shoes and perceive things from his own perspective.

How can you develop empathy?

Here are concrete steps that would help you develop your empathic trait.

Step #1 = Learn how to 'feel' your emotions

This is the first thing that you must learn to do. Unless you are able to recognize your own emotions and feelings, you couldn't relate to the feelings of other people. How do happiness, loneliness and despair feel? Delve inside yourself.

Step #2 – Learn how to put yourself in somebody else's shoes

Put yourself in another person's shoes. So, whenever you observe someone expressing his emotions, try to put yourself in his shoes. What would you feel if you were in his place?

Step #3 – Practice empathy with your family members and friends

At this stage, you can now work with your family members and friends. Practice empathy with them daily. You can do it without them knowing, or you can enlist their help openly.

Step #4 – Practice empathy using TV shows

You can start by watching TV dramas and feeling what the characters in the drama feel. Visualize yourself being the character. Why does the character say the things he says? Imagine yourself being in his place. What you would feel too if you were the character. Let's say he's happy because his mother had undergone a surgical operation successfully.

Visualize yourself seeing your own mother undergoing a successful operation. That would be the emotions the person is experiencing at the moment. Now, you know how he feels. And when you do, you could understand him better.

Step#5 – Practice empathy with strangers

You can now broaden your sphere of empathy by practicing your empathy with persons you don't know. Observe people in mourning and learn how to empathize with them. Observe people who are talking and empathize with them. Try to connect the statements of the persons to their facial expressions and body language.

Be courageous to go out of your comfort zone and practice the trait of empathy. Constant use of your empathic trait would make it easier for you to empathize with people. Once you empathize with people, you will be able to read their minds and actions easier.

Chapter 15: Proven Techniques: Developing Listening Skills

Listening is one of the most important skills that anyone must master in order to have a quality relationship and successful career. People use the skill to obtain information, to understand and to learn. Listening is entirely different from hearing. Hearing is simply a passive form of receiving information without necessarily understanding the message.

When a person listens, he actively takes not only the spoken words but also the body language of the speaker. It may seem to be a simple task, but not all people are good at it. In fact, research suggests that only 25 to 50% of the things we hear are energetically processed in the brain and the rest as they say "goes out to the other ear". For you to become an active listener; here are the things that you must understand.

Listening is a cognitive process. It requires thinking and complex processing of information. Your full concentration is needed to get the most from a conversation. Although multitasking is common nowadays, this is detrimental to active listening. If you wish to fully analyze the person talking in front of you, train your brain to focus its energy on the speaker and all the cues that come with it. Your undivided attention is the key in understanding the speaker and his message better.

Listening situation varies. No two listening situations are exactly the same. Many of its components may change like the speaker, message, timing, place, emotional bond and physiologic factor. For example, hunger, room set-up, relationship of the speaker to the listener, and time of conversation affect the person's ability to comprehend a message. Given these factors, you need to consider these variables when analyzing the communication process as they can have either a negative or a positive impact on your listening abilities. A good listener must be able to adjust to whatever situation and should consider the environment when making an analysis.

Listening must set aside personal biases. Everyone comes from a different background. Your personal experiences may not be the same as the speaker. In active listening, you must be able to manage your own feelings during the situation. Otherwise, your likes and dislikes might come in the context of understanding the other person and they may limit your ability to fully comprehend the message. To be an effective listener, you need to be aware of your own biases and know how they can cause you problems. When you know these things, you will have the idea on how to manage them as you listen to the person talking to you.

Listening requires the use of other senses. Listening is not just about the use of the sense of hearing, but it's the maximum use of the other senses - especially the eyes. Maintaining eye contact with the speaker has several benefits. First of all, it ensures that your attention remains with the speaker and it takes you away from possible distractions. Although there a few exceptions, most cultures around the world consider eye contact as a sign of attentiveness during communication. When you look at the speaker in the eyes, you also get to assess the honesty in his words.

Aside from the eyes, you may also use your hands to take down important notes and to show approval, when necessary.

Listening is a two-way process. When you are asked to listen, you are also expected to give feedback. However, never interrupt the person in the middle of his speech. Interruption brings frustration on the speaker and limits the full delivery of the information. Wait for the right time to give your comments or reflections about his statements. The speaker will most likely prompt you when it's time to give your views. Be open and honest with your opinion. You may disagree with the speaker but convey your differences with respect.

Listening utilizes body language. Your body language speaks louder than your voice. As a listener, you must also be conscious of how your body speaks about you. Be aware that your actions while listening may give the impression of boredom or eagerness. Fidgeting, tapping a pencil, looking at your wrist watch and engaging in other activities may show disinterest in the topic. Nodding, facial expressions and your posture say a lot about your level of concentration. Some individuals have mannerisms that may annoy the other person. If you are to be a good listener, you must always be conscious about how your body speaks.

In order to better understand a person and improve your relationships, your communication skills must be enhanced, and it all starts by becoming an active listener. Becoming a good listener comes with practice. You have to start today, and once it becomes a habit, you will have less conflicts, better relationships and a wider social circle. You will be able to evaluate people in a different perspective and in a more objective way.

Chapter 16:   Proven Techniques: Effective Profiling

Effective profiling techniques are simply techniques in discovering the genuine personalities of individuals.

When you do a profiling of an individual, you gather all available data and established behavior to find out his personality.

Here are steps in effectively profiling a person.

Technique 1

Step #1 – Prepare a logbook for your activity

You have to record your observations, so that you can refer to them later on.

Step #2 – Observe the person you want to profile

Before the person acts and speaks, what does he do first? What are the common things that he does beforehand?

Step #3 – Observe the person's behavior while he's talking

What are his mannerisms? How does he pronounce words? What are the expressions on his face while he speaks?

Step #5 – Observe the person's behavior after the conversation.

Observe his actions and the way he conducts himself. What are his facial expressions?

Sep #6 - Find patterns in his behavior

You can now find patterns in his behavior that is common in all of the phases of his activities. These common patterns will identify his type of personality.

Technique 2

Step #1 – Observe the person daily

Every day, observe the person you want to profile. You may want to do this discreetly, so that the person won't feel self-conscious. Record all your observations. Don't miss anything. Write down all of your observations on the following:

- Facial expressions
- Outward or external appearance (dress, posture, manner of walking, and similar aspects)
- Body language
- Verbal cues
- Nonverbal cues
- Micro expressions (if you have the chance to get close to him)

Step #2 – Find a pattern

Peruse all the observations you have compiled and find a pattern or patterns. What occurs constantly in his behavior? What's the common denominator in your record? Search for these patterns and use these data to analyze what type of personality he has.

Step #3 – Finalize his type of personality

Based on you patterns, you can now identify the type of personality the individual has. You can use the types of personalities that were mentioned in the previous chapters to determine his type.

Be confident in your decision because you have performed the
steps correctly.

After you have mastered these techniques, it would help you
too in analyzing successfully the personality types of people.

Chapter 17: Proven Techniques in Analyzing People

The previous chapters have presented proven techniques in enhancing your ability to analyze people's personalities. Analyzing people is under the science of psychology. Experts spend years in learning the various ways to get into a person's mind, heart and soul, without them explicitly opening up to others. If you wish to have a deeper understanding of people, you need to know the various ways to gain access to their inner person.

Nevertheless, to help you advance more in your endeavor, here are additional proven techniques in analyzing people.

1. **Combine first impression, intuition and physiognomy**

   When you are not given ample time to analyze a person, you can use these techniques: intuition, first impression, and physiognomy. These were discussed in chapters 6 and 13.

2. **Combine profiling, verbal, nonverbal cues, and Myers-Briggs technique**

   In cases when you have ample time to study the person you're going to analyze, you can do profiling. Observe her verbal and nonverbal cues. Then use the Myers-Briggs Type Indicator (MBTI). These are all discussed in chapters 5, 7, 11, 17.

   To summarize Myers-Briggs technique, you can simply determine the person's:

   Decision making process - Is he Thinking (T) or merely Feeling (F). Which among the two does he use?

Attention focus - is he inclined to Introversion (I), or Extroversion (E)? Being an introvert involves being independent, while extroverts love company. You can go back to chapter 5 to know more.

Dealing with the world - is he quick to Judging (J), or is he simply Perceiving (P)?

Information Acquisition - is he obtaining information through Sensing (S), or through his Intuition (I)?

By answering these questions based on your observation of the individual, you would be able to analyze the individual's personality accurately.

3. Combine all the techniques

The best is to combine all of the techniques, so you can rule out false impressions and confirm the true personality of the individual. This would be a complete analysis of the person. Make use of all the methods presented in this book.

You can also do it individually, such as:

4. Analyze people by their words

Words represent the thoughts of a person. It serves as a gateway to his mind. The use of words is a reflection of the personality and behavior of an individual. For example, you can easily spot a well-educated and mannered person compared with someone uneducated through their language.

Individuals who possess wisdom in life usually engage in profound discussions, while uneducated persons go with shallow talks. By analyzing the choice of words, you get a clue of the traits of a person that could allow you to read their thoughts even without their knowledge. When you practice this method, you need to learn how to read between the lines. Take note of the words they keep on repeating and the words they emphasize during the conversation. The changes in intonation can give you a clue of the message they wish to highlight. These will give you a hint of their hidden emotions and intentions.

5. Analyze people by their handwriting

Another effective and traditional way to analyze people's traits is by looking at their handwriting. Graphology, the science of analyzing the handwriting, is used to get a glimpse of the personality of an individual. Thousands of personality traits can be revealed using the person's handwriting. The size of the letters, slanting, pressure, connections of letters, line spacing, writing "t's, i's, y's and other upper and lower zone letters can tell a lot about a person.

For example, people who have large handwriting are people-oriented, whereas those whose handwritings slant to the right are impulsive, sentimental and friendly. By engaging in graphology, you can have a clue on what to expect from people even without seeing them personally.

6. Analyze People by their Body Language

The body language speaks louder than words. The nonverbal communication is often neglected by individuals but it is actually a gateway to revealing their personalities. Observing the body signals that people send out unconsciously can reveal their inner intention. Anxiety can be conveyed by fidgeting, increased blinking, uneasy body movements and jittery legs. Anger can be exemplified by wide eyes, arms tightly crossed over the other and eyebrow movement. Pride is shown by small smile, hands on the hips and tilting the head backward. By knowing some of these signs, you can actually see a person's characteristics.

7. Analyze People by their Eye Movements

The eyes can give away your secrets and personal information even without your consent. Remember that you cannot hide anything from a person who knows how to analyze eye movements. Rapid movements indicate impulsiveness, whereas slow movement shows fatigue. If you lack or avoid eye contact, this may indicate lying and when you try to look down while talking, feeling of shyness or embarrassment may be assumed. Because of the various movements a person can make with the eyes, listeners can gain access to their mind by simply analyzing them.

8. Analyze People by their Interests

People have different likes and dislikes. Pay attention to the person's activities and hobbies. Try to know what they do during their spare time. Do they go to church, engage in community activities, go to the gym, socialize in parties or stay at home and sleep? These activities will help you understand the nature of the person you are trying to analyze.

What a person does during their free time can tell you about their character and personality. You can also analyze their motivation for doing such activities and help you come up with conclusions about a person's priorities and traits. For example, a person who finds time to exercise despite the busy schedule will give you a clue that he values his health or physical looks.

9. Analyze People by their Culture

Culture can leave a permanent mark in people's personalities. People act and behave according to how they perceive things as "normal" and this is basically motivated by their culture.

When analyzing people, you should consider the person's background. Know where they came from and their traditions. Their values, beliefs, attitude and behavior can be shaped by their culture. With the increased globalization nowadays, it is very common to find people who come from different geographical boundaries. Each of these individuals brings with them the principles that they have been imprinted with. When you analyze their characteristics, consider their familial upbringing, community experiences and other practices that may have significantly influenced them.

10. Analyze People by their Friends

Birds of the same feather flock together. If you wish to know the characteristics of a person, try looking at his friends. They can give you a lot of information. People associate with a certain crowd for a reason. Either they feel comfortable with them or they match his interests. By nature, humans have the tendency to like people who are more like them.

Some also say that you are an average of the five people you spend the most time with. When a person spends time with another, there is an unconscious repetition of the way they behave. They tend to act in the same manner as their friends. This means that if the person you are trying to analyze has an arrogant social circle, expect pride to be his dominating character.

The various ways of analyzing people does not come easily. It requires skills, and most of the time, practice to master them. But once you learn each of them, it becomes second nature to you. Understanding people is crucial for successful relationships and it helps you predict a person's behavior in future circumstances. But as a reminder, always use your basic overview of a person's traits with an open mind to better understand his personality.

These are all proven techniques of analyzing people. These are crucial data and information, which would contribute to your success in analyzing people. Maximize their use and optimize the use of this book.

Chapter 18: How to Become a Better Analyzer

You can become a better analyzer if you're willing to go out of your way and practice randomly among people. You have to acquire and develop certain traits that would support you in analyzing people's personality types. Here are the steps you can observe.

Step #1 – Nurture traits that promote your skill in analyzing people

Aside from inculcating the virtue of empathy, you have to nurture these traits as well:

- Patience
- Dedication
- Hard work
- Helpfulness
- Kindness

Of course, if you can cultivate all the good traits then that would be best.

Step #2 – Be positive

Being positive or optimistic in any undertaking will attract positive vibes and increase your chances of success. Thus, have a positive frame of mind, no matter what the circumstances are. There's always something good in any given situation.

Step #3 – Establish a good reason for your analysis of people

Certainly, you're doing this activity for a good purpose, right? You're not only analyzing people because you enjoy it. You may want to create a noble purpose, such as helping people understand themselves and overcome their problems.

Through your analysis, people could also use this knowledge to learn how to improve their relationships with other people. They could achieve happiness too.

When you have a noble purpose, it motivates you more to improve your skill and do your best.

Naturally, you must consider also your personal purpose, which is to improve your own relationships and to determine people, who are honest to you.

Step #4 – Love what you do

It is only when you truly love what you're doing that you can become better at it. This goes true with analyzing people. You must enjoy analyzing people and helping them afterwards, and you'll surely become better at what you do.

Step #5 – Be self-confident

Believe in yourself because if you don't, nobody else will. Be self-confident that you can master the craft. It's a skill, so with dedication and hard work, you will definitely become proficient and competent. Half of the victory is won if you have faith in yourself.

Step #6 – Practice every day

Practice daily. It's only when you practice the skill that you can get better. Look at all the gymnasts, skaters and other sports players who practice endlessly. Most of them started since they were kids, and the end result? – They excel in what they do. You can be a master too of your own craft (analyzing people), by practicing every chance you get.

These are the steps you can observe to make you a better analyzer of people's personalities. Follow them religiously and you will surely succeed.

Chapter 19:   8 Valuable Tips in Analyzing People

To complete your knowledge, here are valuable tips that can guide you in analyzing people and their personalities.

1. **Don't jump to conclusions**. However, don't dwell too long before making a decision. Learn how to analyze carefully and correctly, but promptly, as well.

2. **There will always be exceptions to the rule.** Take note of these individuals and analyze them appropriately. An example is a pathological liar, who can display wrong nonverbal cues.

3. **Know when to devise and modify the technique to suit your situation.** Rules and procedures are there for you to follow. Nonetheless, you're not a robot. If the situation demands it; modify the rule according to your case. There are instances when a case to case basis must be applied.

4. **Don't stereo type people or make generalizations.** This is one 'sin' that you must never do. Each individual is unique on his own - but just like fingerprints – there are no two identical individuals, with exactly the same traits, physical built and behavior.

   There were claims of 2 persons having the same fingerprints, but on closer look, they would have some differences for sure. Some experts claim that the chance of finding two identical fingerprints is one in 64 billion. The world population is only more than 7 billion.

5. **Treat the persons you're analyzing with respect.** No matter what the circumstances are when you're analyzing people, always treat them with respect. They're human beings and not animals that you're experimenting on.

   In retrospect, the mere fact that you're analyzing them without their consent can be a subject of debate, whether it's morally ethical or not. However, since your goal is to help them and yourself, then it's worth a try.

6. **Learn to utilize your knowledge for the good of everyone.** It is only when you do that you can be good to yourself too. You're here in this world not for yourself alone, but for others too. Extend help whenever you can and you would be happier than the man who doesn't.

7. **Through all the techniques, you must try to understand your mind.** Recognize the role of your mind (brain) in your activity. You won't be able to succeed unless you understand the crucial role your mind plays.

8. **Practice makes perfect**. As the cliché goes: Correct practice makes perfect. All of the techniques presented in this book would be useless, if you don't practice and apply them. So, keep practicing until you master the skill.

These are the 8 tips that you must remember. Life is not only about you and your endeavor of analyzing people's personalities. Life is also about the person you're analyzing; his thoughts, problems and actions.

Conclusion

This book has provided you the basic and proven techniques in analyzing people. Through the various techniques, you would understand how valuable the human mind is. You would also know that the analysis of people starts with you. Analyze yourself first; what is your personality type? And then go on from there.

The personalities of people differ from one another and, often, verbal and nonverbal language cause inevitable clashes. But through your skill, you can help settle diffcrences and promote harmonious relationships. Make people happy.

Be the ambassador of goodwill through your mastery of analyzing people.

www.ingramcontent.com/pod-product-compliance
Lightning Source LLC
Chambersburg PA
CBHW070820240726
48654CB00007B/413